# Titles in This Series:

Jungle Babies
Farm Friends
Pets, Pets, Pets
Little Birds, Big Birds

# ◆Animals and Their Babies◆

# Little Birds, Big Birds

Text by Henry Mangione
Illustrations by Nemo and Bertello

## A Little Simon Book

Published by Simon & Schuster, Inc.
New York

Created and manufactured by arrangement with Ottenheimer Publishers, Inc.
Copyright © 1987 by Ottenheimer Publishers, Inc.
All rights reserved including the right of reproduction in whole or in part in any form.
Published by LITTLE SIMON, a division of Simon & Schuster, Inc.,
Simon & Schuster Building, 1230 Avenue of the Americas, New York, New York 10020.
LITTLE SIMON and colophon are trademarks of Simon & Schuster, Inc.
Manufactured in Hong Kong.
10 9 8 7 6 5 4 3 2 1
ISBN 0-671-63491-7

# Sparrows

Sparrows are small seed-eating birds. Farmers think sparrows are terrible pests because they like to eat up all their seeds, grains, and fruits. Not even scarecrows can keep sparrows away.

When sparrows find a place they like, they stay for a long time. Sparrows build nests quickly, but if they have to, they will also live in nests that other birds have left.

Even though sparrows do a lot of damage, they also eat insects and other pests that are even worse.

Both mother and father sparrows take good care of their babies. They bring them food to eat all day long, and when the babies are strong enough, both mother and father teach them how to fly. Young sparrows leave the nest as soon as they can fly well.

# Peacocks

Peacocks are very proud birds, and they like to walk around showing off their beautiful feathers. Even young peacocks, who do not have their colors yet, like to show off. Young peacocks don't begin to grow their beautiful tails until they are a month old.

Mother peacocks are called peahens. They are not as brightly colored as the males. Peahens are very gentle, but they will defend their chicks against anything that might harm them.

Peacocks use their shiny tails to impress peahens, to show when they are angry, and when they are hungry, too.

Peacocks have full tails and colors when they are three years old. In India people think peacock tails have magic powers.

# Lady Amherst's Pheasant

Lady Amherst's Pheasants live high in the mountains of the Tibetan highlands near China. They only come down into the valleys in winter when food is scarce.

In the spring, the pheasants go back into the mountains to lay their eggs. Mother pheasants are very smart. When the air is cool they sit on the eggs, but when the sun is warm they leave to find food. The newly hatched chicks look like tiny balls of feathers, but soon they will grow into beautiful birds like their parents, with white tipped wings and long feathers.

Pheasant chicks grow quickly. As babies, they like to eat grubs and insects, but as they grow up, pheasants will eat only berries and seeds.

# Rhinoceros Hornbill

The Rhinoceros hornbill is a relative of the woodpecker. The hornbill lives in warm, tropical areas. Hornbills have a strange, horny beak which is where they get their name. Hornbills do not fly much because their wings are clumsy and make lots of noise.

These birds build very unusual nests. The mother digs a hole in a hollow tree and goes inside. Then the father seals off the hole with mud. Only a small hole is left open. The father passes food through this tiny opening to the mother for the whole three months she stays inside. The mother lays her eggs and the chicks grow up safe inside the tree. After a while the parents break open the nest so the babies can learn to fly.

When they can fly, the young hornbills go off to find homes of their own.

# Ostrich

Ostriches can run very fast. Their long, powerful legs are made especially for running because they can't fly. That means they must have another way to escape from their enemies. Ostriches use their wings for balance. Their feet are big and have claws, and are dangerous weapons. Ostriches can turn their heads in all directions on their long necks to look for danger.

Ostriches live in groups, and they lay their eggs all together in a hole. Baby ostriches, called chicks, can run as soon as they are born, and soon learn to handle the dangers of the grasslands.

Ostriches are friendly with other animals such as baboons, gazelles, giraffes, and zebras, and often warn them when danger is near.

# Crowned Crane

Crowned cranes spend their entire lives in the same pond, or stretch of beach. Each group of cranes has a special language that only that group knows. Crowned cranes also have a special dance that the males do to find mates. The cranes bow and curtsey, then strut backwards and forwards, while fluttering their wings. Then, they hop straight up in the air, almost as if music was playing, and offer each other bits of moss.

Crowned cranes like to eat frogs, insects, and grain. They nest in the reeds and that's where their babies are born. As the babies grow up, they grow the crown of bright feathers, and learn the language and dance of the crane colony.

# Pelican

Pelicans fly in flocks from one place to another looking for fish to eat. They are excellent fishers and scoop the fish up into their neck pouches. Sometimes pelicans will first scare the fish into shallow water where they are easier to catch.

Pelicans make their nests in the reeds. Each female pelican lays about 4 eggs. The chicks are very tiny and have brown feathers. They turn white as they grow older. Mother pelicans chew the food for their babies. The babies stick their beaks into mother's pouch to drink up the mushy, fish soup which is easier to swallow. Soon the baby pelicans are able to catch fish for themselves.

# Bald Eagle

The bald eagle is the national symbol of the United States. This bird is a symbol for bravery and vision. Eagles are powerful flyers and have keen eyesight. They live in nests called eyries. They like to build their nests in trees or in rocky cliffs. They eat reptiles, small mammals, fish, and other birds.

Bald eagles live in North America. They are so big, their wings are sometimes eight feet long from the tip of one wing to the tip of the other.

Baby eagles are born with no feathers. Their feathers grow in when they are two months old. They can fly when they are about four or five months old.

# Blue and Yellow Macaw

Macaws are a kind of parrot that live in South America. They are large birds and have very brightly colored blue and yellow feathers.

There are different kinds of macaws. Some are as small as pigeons. Others are over three feet long. They are easy to keep as pets, but wild macaws can be dangerous if bothered. Their beaks are strong enough to cut off a man's finger!

Macaws are shy and like to live in the highest trees. Baby macaws are very funny-looking, but they grow up to be as pretty as their parents. Macaws used to be hunted a lot, and because of this, there are not many of these beautiful birds left.

# Pigeons

Pigeons make very good parents, and it is said that male and female pigeons love each other very much, and stay together for life. Baby pigeons can fly when they are just six weeks old, and after six months they are full grown.

Pigeon feathers are very loose and will fall out very easily. They have short bills with thick tips. Pigeons belong to the dove family. They are usually soft brown in color. Wood-pigeons are not liked by farmers because they eat up all his seeds and grains.

Pigeons were once used to carry messages from place to place. That is because they can fly long distances and come right back to the place they started from!

# Swallows

Swallows live in most areas of the world where the weather is mild, and farms are nearby. Farmers like swallows because swallows eat as many as 3000 harmful bugs each day. Swallows can fly very fast. They have been known to fly 40 miles an hour.

Swallows lay three to six eggs at a time. The eggs hatch after fifteen days. The parents keep very busy feeding the young swallows. They make about twenty trips an hour, catching bugs to bring back to the hungry babies. After three weeks the chicks are able to fly off and live on their own.

Swallows fly to warmer areas every winter. They return to their nesting areas for spring and summer.

# Swans

Swans are water birds with an almost magical beauty. They are part of many legends and fairy tales all over the world.

A male swan is called a cob and a female is called a pen.

Baby swans, called cygnets, hatch about five weeks after the pen lays her eggs. Cygnets are ugly when they are young, but after four years they grow into beautiful adult swans.

As pretty as they are, swans are unfriendly birds and will hiss when they are angry. They are dangerous if you scare them or threaten their babies. Swans use their long necks to pick snails, their favorite food, off river beds.